W9-AWJ-605

LOCUST VALLEY LIBRARY

# INTRODUCTION

Yellowstone was our nation's first national park.
There are over 10,000 geysers in Yellowstone
  Park.
Old Faithful is the most famous of them all.
Old Faithful has become a world symbol for the
  preservation of wilderness.

# I AM AN ARO PUBLISHING
# 40 WORD BOOK

## MY 40 WORDS ARE:

| | |
|---|---|
| A | moose |
| all | me |
| air | Old Faithful |
| buffalo | really |
| be | ran |
| Bubba | run |
| bear | see |
| blows | said |
| behind | sniffing |
| big | scare |
| don't (do not) | time |
| every | to |
| go   goes | there |
| hour | the |
| I | tree |
| it | then |
| is | we'll (we will) |
| it's  (it is) | where |
| late | when |
| Mickey | won't (will not) |

© Copyright 1986 by Aro Publishing Co. All rights reserved, including the right of reproduction in whole or in part in any form. Designed and produced by Aro Publishing Co. Printed in the U.S.A. P.O. Box 193 Provo, Utah 84603.
ISBN 0-89868-167-7 — Library Bound
ISBN 0-89868-168-5 — Soft Bound

YELLOWSTONE CRITTERS

# OLD FAITHFUL

## BY BOB REESE

ARO PUBLISHING

"It's time to see," said buffalo.

"Don't be late. It's time to go."

"It's time to see," said Bubba Bear.

"Don't be late. We'll all be there."

Mickey Moose said, sniffing the air,

" don't be late. We'll all be where?"

"To see Old Faithful, when it goes.
Every hour it really blows."

Buffalo said, "It's time to see."

**Buffalo ran behind a tree!**

Bubba Bear said, "It's time to see."

**Bubba Bear ran behind a tree!**

Mickey Moose said, "It won't scare me.

I won't run behind a tree."

"Old Faithful is big. It really goes.

**Every hour it really blows!"**

**Mickey Moose said, "It won't scare me."**

Then Mickey Moose ran behind a tree!

2216 00060 2999